THE ART OF PEACEFUL LIVING

VANDANA SINGH

With deepest gratitude, I extend my sincere appreciation to all my guides and mentors, whose wisdom and support have helped me embark on a journey of self-discovery. Their profound insights have been a beacon of light, guiding me toward clarity, inner peace, and a deeper understanding of life. The encouragement and trust instilled through their teachings have played a pivotal role in shaping this book, and for that, I am forever grateful.

Contents

Preface

My Journey to Peaceful Living

I wrote this book while preparing for one of the toughest exams in India—the **UPSC Civil Services Examination**. Like many others, I faced moments of self-doubt, procrastination, emotional turmoil, and difficulties in managing relationships.

There were nights when **overthinking stole my sleep**, days when distractions consumed my study hours, and moments when I felt **lost in seeking validation from others**. I realized that **success isn't just about hard work—it's about inner peace, emotional stability, and resilience.**

This book is not just about UPSC preparation. It is about **mastering life**—learning to:

- Overcome overthinking and procrastination
- Stay emotionally stable in tough situations
- Build meaningful yet detached relationships
- Manage time wisely and study smartly
- Find joy in solitude and self-fulfillment

Each chapter contains **real-life experiences, powerful techniques, and motivational quotes** that transformed my journey. I hope it helps you find your **own path to success—peaceful and fulfilling.**

Acknowledgements

This book is a reflection of my journey through struggles, self-discovery, and the pursuit of success. I express my deepest gratitude to **everyone who has been a part of my journey**—my family, friends, mentors, and even those challenges that tested my patience and strength.

To all the **UPSC aspirants and dreamers** out there, this book is for you. May it help you navigate your struggles with peace, confidence, and clarity.

CHAPTER I

The Power of Self-Awareness

"Knowing yourself is the beginning of all wisdom." — Aristotle

---

Why Self-Awareness is the First Step to Success

During my UPSC journey, I often found myself **frustrated, impatient, and emotionally overwhelmed.** Sometimes I would doubt my abilities; other times, I would get too attached to people and lose focus on my studies.

One day, I asked myself:

- *Why do I react this way?*
- *Why do I feel restless when I study alone?*
- *Why do I seek attention or approval from others?*

That's when I realized: **I was unaware of my own mind and emotions.**

Self-awareness is **not just about knowing who you are**—it's about understanding **why you think, feel, and act the way you do.** Once you become aware of your inner patterns, you gain **control over your emotions, relationships, and focus.**

The "Pause & Observe" Technique

The biggest mistake we make is **reacting without thinking.** Whether it's getting angry, feeling insecure, or overthinking, we act **impulsively.**

To change this, I started using the **"Pause & Observe"** technique:

- **Step 1:** The moment I felt angry, frustrated, or distracted, I **paused for 5 seconds**.
- **Step 2:** Instead of reacting immediately, I **observed my thoughts** without judging them.
- **Step 3:** I asked myself: *"Is this thought helpful? Will this reaction solve anything?"*
- **Step 4:** If the answer was *no*, I chose **not to react emotionally**.

This simple habit **saved me from unnecessary conflicts, emotional breakdowns, and distractions**.

Story: The UPSC Aspirant Who Lost His Peace

There was a UPSC aspirant named **Rohit**. He was intelligent but had a habit of comparing himself with others. Whenever his friends discussed mock test scores, he felt **inferior**.

One day, he scored **low in a test** and started overthinking:
"What if I never clear UPSC? What will people say?"

He became restless, procrastinated, and wasted days in self-doubt.

One of his mentors advised him:
*"Rohit, you are not failing because of low marks—you are failing because of your **emotional reactions**. Learn to observe your thoughts instead of getting controlled by them."*

Rohit started practicing **self-awareness**. Whenever negative thoughts arose, he paused and asked:
"Is this thought helping me? Or is it just fear?"

Slowly, he stopped **overreacting to failures** and started focusing on consistent improvement. In his **third attempt, he cleared UPSC**.

a. **Lesson:** The problem is not failure; the problem is **how we react to it**.

How to Apply Self-Awareness in Daily Life

1. *Journal Your Thoughts Daily*

Every night, write down:

- What emotions did I feel today?
- What made me stressed or distracted?
- What can I do better tomorrow?

2. Name Your Emotions

- Instead of saying *"I feel bad"*, say *"I feel frustrated because I couldn't complete my study target."*
- This helps in **understanding the real issue**.

3. Accept Without Judgment

- Instead of feeling guilty for overthinking, say: *"It's okay. I will work on it."*
- Self-awareness is about **observing, not blaming**.

Key Takeaways

Before we can succeed in **UPSC or life**, we must first **understand ourselves**. The more aware you become, the more control you gain over your **emotions, focus, and happiness**.

CHAPTER II

Breaking Free from Overthinking

"Overthinking is the art of creating problems that don't exist."

The Trap of Overthinking
During my UPSC journey, I often found myself **lost in thoughts**:

- *What if I don't clear the exam?*
- *What will people say if I fail?*
- *Am I studying the right way?*

Instead of focusing on the **present** and **studying**, my mind was trapped in endless loops of **"what ifs" and "maybes"**. Overthinking didn't solve any problems—it only created stress, self-doubt, and procrastination.

One day, I realized: **Overthinking is not thinking—it's wasting mental energy on things beyond control.**

If you are an **overthinker**, this chapter will help you **break free from mental loops and focus on action.**

The "STOP" Method to Control Overthinking

Whenever I found myself overthinking, I used the **STOP method**:

- **S – See the thought:** Pause and recognize when you're overthinking.
- **T – Take a deep breath:** Deep breathing helps to regain control.
- **O – Observe without reacting:** Ask, *"Is this thought helping me?"*

- **P – Proceed with action:** Shift focus to **solving the problem** instead of thinking about it.

Story: The Girl Who Overthought Her UPSC Exam

Priya was a hardworking UPSC aspirant. She studied for hours but was **constantly worried** about failure.

Instead of revising, she spent **hours thinking**:

- *"What if the paper is too tough?"*
- *"What if I don't clear Prelims?"*
- *"Should I change my study strategy?"*

Her friend advised her:
"Priya, worrying won't change the outcome. Just focus on **what you can do today.**"

She started using the **STOP method** and replaced overthinking with **studying smarter**. On exam day, instead of panicking, she **trusted her preparation and performed well.**

a. **Lesson:** Overthinking only **wastes time—action brings results.**

How to Stop Overthinking in Daily Life

u. **1. Set a "Thinking Time"**

- If you tend to overthink, set a **fixed time (10-15 min daily)** to analyze your worries.
- After that, **stop dwelling on them and move to action.**

u. **2. Focus on the Present Moment**

- When you catch yourself overthinking, bring your attention to **what you are doing NOW**.
- Example: If you are studying, remind yourself: *"Right now, my only job is to study."*

u. **3. Shift from Problem to Solution**

- Instead of thinking *"What if I fail?"*, ask *"What can I do now to improve my chances?"*
- Overthinking keeps you stuck—solutions move you forward.

Key Takeaways

Your thoughts create your reality. If you focus on problems, you create stress. If you focus on solutions, you create success.

CHAPTER III

Emotional Stability in Challenging Situations

"Calmness is a superpower. The more you control your emotions, the stronger you become.

Why Emotional Stability Matters

Life is unpredictable. Whether it's **failing an exam, losing relationships, or facing criticism,** challenges are bound to come. But what makes the difference is **how we react to them.**

During my UPSC preparation, I often felt:

- **Frustrated** when I couldn't meet my study targets.
- **Angry** when people doubted my abilities.
- **Hurt** when I felt ignored or misunderstood.

Every time something negative happened, my emotions took over, and I **reacted impulsively**—either by arguing, crying, or overthinking.

But over time, I realized that **reacting emotionally only made things worse.** Instead of solving problems, I ended up feeling drained, distracted, and unhappy.

That's when I decided: **I will train myself to be emotionally stable.**

My Struggles: How I Let Emotions Control Me

I have lost **valuable relationships** because of my **own emotional instability**.

Whenever I felt insecure, I became **possessive**.
Whenever I doubted someone's care, I became **demanding**.
Whenever I felt ignored, I became **angry and impatient**.

I didn't realize it then, but my **own thoughts and reactions** were pushing away the people who genuinely cared for me. Instead of **trusting and understanding**, I let **fears, doubts, and insecurities ruin everything**.

One day, after another emotional breakdown, I sat alone and asked myself:

- *"Is this the life I want? Do I want to be controlled by my emotions forever?"*
  The answer was **NO**.

I decided to **change myself**—not for others, but for my own peace and happiness.

The "3-Second Rule" to Control Emotional Reactions

To stop myself from reacting impulsively, I started using the **3-Second Rule**:

- **Step 1:** When I felt a strong emotion (anger, sadness, frustration), I took **3 deep breaths** before responding.
- **Step 2:** I asked myself: *"Is this reaction going to help me or harm me?"*
- **Step 3:** If the reaction was negative, I **chose silence or a calm response instead**.

This simple method **saved me from unnecessary conflicts and regrets.**

Story: The Aspirant Who Let His Emotions Destroy Him

Amit was a brilliant UPSC aspirant. But he had one major weakness—**he couldn't handle criticism.**

Whenever someone pointed out his mistakes, he got **defensive and angry.** He felt like people were attacking him.

During a mock interview, his mentor gave him feedback:
"Your answers lack depth. You need to improve your reasoning skills."

Instead of taking it positively, Amit got **offended** and stopped attending mock sessions.

On the final interview day, he faced tough questions but couldn't handle them well. **He failed.**

- After his failure, Amit realized:
  "I failed not because I lacked knowledge, but because I let my emotions control me."

In his next attempt, he worked on **his emotional stability,** accepted feedback with an open mind, and performed exceptionally well. **This time, he cleared the exam.**

a. **Lesson:** Emotional stability is just as important as knowledge.

How to Stay Emotionally Stable in Daily Life

1. Practice the "3-Second Rule"

- Before reacting, pause for **3 seconds**, breathe, and **respond calmly**.

2. Stop Taking Things Personally

- Most people's actions are **not about you**, but about them.
- Instead of feeling hurt, ask: *"Is this really worth my peace?"*

3. Accept What You Can't Control

- Not everything will go your way, and that's okay.
- Instead of fighting reality, **adapt and move forward.**

Key Takeaways: Finding Inner Peace

Today, I am **calmer, happier, and emotionally stable.** I no longer let my emotions **control my actions or decisions.**

- I don't get attached to people in an unhealthy way.
- I don't let failures break my confidence.
- I don't waste time overreacting to small problems.

This journey of emotional stability has **transformed my relationships, my mindset, and my approach to success.**
And I want the same for you. **Master your emotions, and you will master your life.**

CHAPTER IV

The Secret to Self-Discipline & Overcoming Procrastination

"You will never always be motivated, so you must learn to be disciplined."

Why Self-Discipline is the Key to Success

During my UPSC preparation, I struggled a lot with **procrastination**.

I would plan my study schedule, but when the time came to study, my mind would make excuses:

- *"I'll start in 10 minutes."*
- *"Let me check my phone first."*
- *"I'll study harder tomorrow."*

Before I knew it, hours had passed, and I had wasted valuable time. This cycle repeated itself, leaving me **stressed, guilty, and behind schedule.**

- One day, I realized:
  "If I keep waiting for motivation, I will never get things done. I need discipline, not just inspiration."

That's when I made the decision to **break free from procrastination and develop self-discipline.**

My Struggle: How Procrastination Delayed My Progress

There were days when I would sit with my books but **not actually study.**

I would read a few lines, then get distracted, then scroll through my phone, then overthink about the future. I was **busy but not productive.**

I kept convincing myself that I had "plenty of time" to study properly later. But when the exam date got closer, I realized **how much time I had wasted.**

I wasn't failing because I lacked intelligence—I was failing because I lacked **discipline and consistency.**

That's when I decided: **No more excuses. No more delaying. I will train myself to stay disciplined.**

The "5-Minute Rule" to Overcome Procrastination

To fight procrastination, I started using the **5-Minute Rule:**

- **Step 1:** Whenever I didn't feel like studying, I told myself, *"Just study for 5 minutes."*
- **Step 2:** *Once I started, I usually continued for much longer.*
- **Step 3:** Even if I stopped after 5 minutes, at least I had made progress.

This simple trick helped me break the habit of **waiting for motivation** and instead, focus on **starting immediately.**

Story: The Aspirant Who Waited for Motivation

Rahul was an intelligent UPSC aspirant, but he had one weakness—**he only studied when he felt motivated.**

Some days, he would study for 10 hours straight. Other days, he wouldn't study at all because he "wasn't in the mood."

As the exam approached, he realized he had **huge gaps in his preparation.** He panicked, tried to cover everything at once, but it was too late. He couldn't clear the exam.

The next year, Rahul changed his approach. Instead of relying on motivation, he focused on **discipline.** He set **fixed study hours,** followed a routine, and used the **5-Minute Rule** whenever he felt like procrastinating.

This time, he cleared the exam with confidence.

? **Lesson:** Motivation is temporary, but discipline creates success.

How to Build Self-Discipline in Daily Life

1. Set a Fixed Study Routine

- Decide your study hours and follow them **no matter what.**

2. Use the "5-Minute Rule"

- If you feel like procrastinating, just **start for 5 minutes.**

3. Remove Distractions

- Keep your phone away while studying.
- Use apps like **Forest** or **Pomodoro Timer** to stay focused.

4. Track Your Progress

- Maintain a **study journal** to see your daily progress.
- Seeing improvement keeps you motivated.

Key Takeaways: Progress Over Perfection

I won't say I never procrastinate anymore. There are still days when I feel lazy or distracted.

But now, I know how to **manage it and get back on track quickly.** Instead of waiting for the perfect mood, I **just start, stay consistent, and push through distractions.**

Self-discipline is not about being perfect—it's about making progress **every single day.** Even small efforts, when done consistently, lead to great results.

And that's what I want you to remember. **Start today, stay disciplined, and success will follow.**

CHAPTER V

How to Find Peace, Happiness, and Self-Satisfaction from Within

---

"Happiness is not something you find—it's something you create within yourself."

Why We Seek Happiness Outside

For a long time, I believed that happiness depended on **people, achievements, or external things.**

- *"I will be happy when I clear UPSC."*
- *"I will be happy if people appreciate me."*
- *"I will be happy when I have a perfect relationship."*

But no matter what I achieved, I always felt like **something was missing.** Even when I was surrounded by people, I felt **lonely inside.**

- That's when I asked myself:
  "If happiness depends on something outside, will I ever be truly happy?"
- The answer was **NO.**

I realized that **peace and happiness have to come from within—not from achievements, relationships, or validation.**

My Struggle: Depending on Others for Happiness

I used to rely too much on **people's presence, attention, and opinions** to feel good about myself.

- If someone praised me, I felt happy.
- If someone ignored me, I felt hurt.
- If I was alone, I felt incomplete.

This dependency made me **emotionally weak and unstable.**

But over time, I learned that true happiness comes when **you don't depend on anyone or anything to feel good.**

I started practicing **self-awareness, self-love, and self-acceptance.** Instead of seeking happiness from outside, I **created it within myself.**

The "Mirror Rule" for Self-Satisfaction

One simple habit helped me build **inner happiness**—I call it the **Mirror Rule:**

- **Step 1:** Every morning, I looked in the mirror and said: *"I am enough. I don't need external validation to be happy."*
- **Step 2:** *Throughout the day, whenever I felt lonely or insecure, I reminded myself: "Happiness is within me, not outside me."*
- **Step 3:** I started enjoying my own company—reading, writing, and sitting in silence without needing distractions.
- This habit made me **strong, independent, and peaceful from within.**

Story: The Woman Who Found Happiness Within

Meera was always dependent on others for happiness.

She needed constant validation from friends, family, and social media. She always worried about what people thought of her.

One day, she lost her closest friend due to misunderstandings. She felt completely **lost and alone.**

At first, she tried to fill the emptiness by seeking new people and distractions. But nothing worked.

Then, she decided to change her approach.

She started spending time alone, meditating, and writing down things she loved about herself. Over time, she realized that **she didn't need anyone else to complete her—she was enough.**

Today, Meera is one of the happiest and most peaceful people. Not because she has a perfect life, but because she has learned to be happy **from within.**

a. **Lesson:** True happiness starts when you stop depending on others for it.

How to Find Peace and Happiness Within

1. Spend Time Alone Without Distractions

- Avoid using social media or seeking people's attention when you feel lonely.
- Sit quietly, read, write, or simply observe your thoughts.

2. Practice Gratitude Every Day

- Every morning, write down **three things you are grateful for.**
- Gratitude shifts your focus from **what's missing** to **what you have.**

3. Stop Seeking External Validation

- Don't wait for people to praise you—**appreciate yourself.**
- If someone ignores you, **it's not your loss—it's their choice.**

4. Enjoy Your Own Company

- Go for a walk alone.
- Have a solo coffee date.
- Do things that make **you** happy, without expecting company.

Key Takeaways: Becoming Peaceful and Self-Satisfied

I won't say I never feel lonely anymore. There are moments when I still crave company. But the difference is that **I no longer depend on it for my happiness.**

Now, I enjoy spending time with people, but I also love **being alone.** I appreciate compliments, but I don't **need them** to feel good.

Happiness is not about **what you have or who is with you—it's about how you feel within yourself.**

And today, I feel **peaceful, self-sufficient, and happy from within.**

CHAPTER VI

Overcoming the Fear of Loneliness and Sleeping Alone Peacefully

---

"You are never truly alone when you are at peace with yourself."

Why Loneliness Feels Scary

For a long time, I was afraid of **being alone.**

- If I had no one to talk to, I felt restless.
- If I had to sleep alone, I overthought everything.
- If people weren't around, I felt empty.

I thought being alone meant **being unwanted or unloved.**

- But one day, I asked myself:
  "Why do I fear being with myself? Shouldn't my own company be enough?"

That question changed everything.
I realized that loneliness is not **about being alone—it's about not being comfortable with yourself.**

My Struggle: Sleeping Alone and Overthinking at Night

Nights were the hardest.

The moment I lay down, my mind started overthinking:

- *"What if something bad happens?"*
- *"What if I make the wrong choices in life?"*
- *"What if I always stay alone?"*

These thoughts made me **anxious and sleepless.**

But I slowly trained my mind to **stop fearing loneliness and enjoy solitude instead.**

The "Nighttime Peace Ritual" to Sleep Without Overthinking

To overcome my fear of sleeping alone, I followed a simple **Nighttime Peace Ritual:**

- **Step 1:** Before sleeping, I wrote down all my worries on paper. This helped me **clear my mind.**
- **Step 2:** I played **calm music** or listened to a guided meditation to relax.
- **Step 3:** I reminded myself: *"I am safe, I am at peace, and I am enough."*
- **Step 4:** I focused on my breath, letting go of all thoughts.

This practice **trained my mind to relax** instead of overthinking at night.

Story: The Girl Who Feared Sleeping Alone

Vrinda always needed someone with her at night. She felt uneasy in silence and overthought every little thing.

But one day, she moved to a new city for work. She had no choice but to sleep alone.

At first, she struggled—she stayed awake for hours, feeling anxious.

But then, she started practicing a **Nighttime Peace Ritual**. She wrote down her thoughts, played soft music, and repeated calming affirmations.

Within a few weeks, she started **sleeping peacefully.** Now, she enjoys her alone time and no longer fears sleeping alone.

a. **Lesson:When you train your mind to feel safe alone, loneliness disappears.**

How to Overcome the Fear of Loneliness and Sleep Peacefully

1. Reframe Loneliness as "Me Time"

- Being alone is not a punishment—it's **a time to relax, reflect, and grow.**

2. Avoid Social Media Before Bed

- Scrolling through social media before sleeping increases overthinking.
- Instead, read a book, write, or listen to peaceful music.

3. Use Positive Affirmations

- Before sleeping, repeat: *"I am safe. I am at peace. I enjoy my own company."*

4. Make Your Bedtime Routine Calming

- Dim the lights, play soft music, and create a **peaceful sleep environment.**

Key Takeaways: Finding Peace in Solitude

I won't say I never feel lonely anymore. But now, I **don't fear it.**

I enjoy my own company. I have learned that being alone **does not mean being incomplete.**

Now, when I sleep alone, I feel **safe, peaceful, and content.**

Because true peace comes **not from others—but from within.**

CHAPTER VII

How to Handle Harsh, Stressful, and Challenging Situations in Real Time

---

"You can't control everything, but you can control how you respond."

Why We Struggle in Difficult Situations

Whenever I faced a harsh or stressful situation, my **first reaction** was usually:

- **Panic** (*"What if I mess up?"*)
- **Anger** (*"Why is this happening to me?"*)
- **Overthinking** (*"How will I handle this?"*)

Instead of solving the problem, I got stuck in **negative emotions.**

- But I slowly realized something important:
  "Life will always throw challenges at me. But I can choose how to respond."

Once I understood this, I started developing **mental strength and emotional stability** to handle tough situations **calmly and effectively.**

My Struggle: Reacting Instead of Responding

There were times when I:

- Got **angry and said things I regretted later.**
- Let **stress affect my performance.**
- Avoided problems instead of **facing them.**

But one incident changed my approach completely.

Story: The Power of a Calm Response

During my UPSC preparation, I once had a heated argument with a close friend.

I was frustrated with my studies, and when she said something small, **I snapped at her.** She got upset and stopped talking to me.

At first, **I justified my anger**—thinking *"I was stressed, she should understand."* But later, I realized that my reaction was **wrong.**

So, instead of letting my ego take over, I calmly apologized. I told her, *"I was frustrated and took it out on you. I shouldn't have done that."*

She understood, and our friendship remained strong.

a. **Lesson:** A calm response **saves relationships, reduces stress, and gives you control over the situation.**

How to Stay Calm and Strong in Stressful Situations

1. Pause Before Reacting

- Take a deep breath before **responding to any harsh situation.**
- This gives you time to think and **respond wisely.**

2. Ask Yourself: "Will This Matter in 5 Years?"

- Most problems feel big in the moment but are **irrelevant in the long run.**
- This perspective helps you stay calm.

3. Focus on Solutions, Not Emotions

- Instead of thinking *"Why is this happening to me?"*, ask **"What can I do next?"**
- A solution-focused mindset reduces stress.

4. Train Your Mind to Accept Uncertainty

- Not everything in life will go as planned.
- Learning to **adapt and move forward** makes you mentally strong.

Key Takeaways: Becoming Emotionally Strong and Stable

I won't say I never feel stressed anymore. But now, I know how to **handle stress without letting it control me.**

- When challenges come, I **pause, think, and respond wisely.**
- When emotions rise, I **stay calm and focus on solutions.**
- When things go wrong, I **accept, adapt, and move forward.**

This simple shift in mindset has made me **stronger, calmer, and more in control of my life.**

CHAPTER VIII

Mastering the Art of Peaceful and Harmonious Relationships

"The quality of your life depends on the quality of your relationships—so learn to nurture them with balance."

Why Relationships Get Messed Up

I used to struggle a lot with relationships—whether it was with friends, family, or mentors.

- Sometimes, I got **too attached** and expected too much.
- Other times, I became **impatient and frustrated** over small things.
- I often **sought too much attention** or tried to control situations.

The result? **Conflicts, misunderstandings, and regrets.**

But over time, I realized that **peaceful relationships are built on balance, understanding, and emotional maturity.**

My Struggle: Hurting People Who Helped Me

There were people in my life who genuinely cared for me, helped me, and wanted the best for me.

But because of my **negative thinking, insecurities, and over-attachment, I:**

- Doubted their intentions.
- Became possessive or overly dependent.

- **Got angry and pushed them away.**

Eventually, I lost many good people.

- This regret **taught me a life lesson**—if I wanted meaningful relationships, I needed to:
- Be **patient and understanding.**
- Be **grateful instead of doubtful.**
- Maintain **healthy emotional boundaries.**

Story: The Girl Who Almost Lost a True Friend

Ananya had a best friend, Riya, who always supported her.

But Ananya had deep insecurities. She overthought every small thing Riya said. If Riya talked to someone else, Ananya felt ignored. If Riya didn't text back quickly, Ananya got upset.

One day, Riya said, *"I feel like I have to prove my friendship to you all the time."*

That's when Ananya realized her mistake. She was **seeking too much validation instead of trusting the friendship.**

She decided to **change her approach**—she gave Riya space, trusted her more, and focused on her own happiness. Their friendship became **stronger and more peaceful.**

a. **Lesson:Don't ruin good relationships by overthinking and seeking too much attention. Give love, trust, and space.**

How to Maintain Peaceful and Harmonious Relationships

1. Learn to Detach Emotionally

- Love people, but don't be overly attached.

- Understand that **everyone has their own life and space.**

2. Respond, Don't React

- Before reacting with anger, **pause and think.**
- Choose calm and understanding over frustration.

3. Stop Seeking Too Much Validation

- Real relationships don't need constant approval.
- Trust that **people who care will stay, even if they don't always show it.**

4. Communicate Honestly Without Ego

- If something bothers you, **talk about it calmly.**
- Don't let small misunderstandings destroy good relationships.

Key Takeaways: Choosing Peace Over Drama

Now, I no longer feel the **urge to control relationships** or seek excessive validation.

- I let people be who they are.
- I trust instead of overthinking.
- I choose **peace and positivity** over unnecessary drama.

This shift has made my relationships **more fulfilling, balanced, and joyful.**

CHAPTER IX

How to Stay Focused on Your Goal and Stop Procrastinating

"Discipline is choosing what you want most over what you want now."

Why We Procrastinate and Lose Focus

I always dreamed of **cracking the UPSC exam,** but I often found myself:

- **Wasting time overthinking** instead of studying.
- **Feeling insecure and doubting myself** instead of taking action.
- **Getting distracted by social media, relationships, or random thoughts.**

I kept telling myself *"I'll start tomorrow,"* but tomorrow never came.

- One day, I asked myself:
  "If I don't focus now, how will my future self feel?"

That thought hit me hard. I realized that **every distraction was stealing my dream.**

My Struggle: Escaping the Cycle of Delay and Regret

I kept delaying my studies, thinking I had **enough time**. But then, deadlines got closer, and my stress increased.

- I felt **guilty for wasting time.**
- I **rushed through topics** instead of understanding them deeply.
- I **doubted my ability** to clear the exam.

This cycle of **procrastination** → **regret** → **stress** became a pattern.

But then, I made a small change that **transformed everything.**

Story: The "5-Minute Rule" That Changed Everything

During my preparation, I read about the **5-Minute Rule:**

"If something feels hard, do it for just 5 minutes. If you want to quit after that, you can."

One day, when I didn't feel like studying, I told myself:
"Just study for 5 minutes—then decide if you want to stop."

To my surprise, after 5 minutes, I felt focused and continued for hours!

a. **Lesson:Starting is the hardest part. Once you start, momentum takes over**

How to Stay Focused and Stop Procrastinating

1. Break Big Tasks into Small, Manageable Steps
   2. Use the 5-Minute Rule
   3. Eliminate Distractions
   4. Stay Reminded of Your "Why"

Key Takeaways: Choosing Discipline Over Regret

Now, I don't let distractions **steal my dreams.**
    And that's how I am turning my **UPSC dream into reality.**

- Instead of saying *"I have to study for 8 hours,"* say *"I will complete one topic first."*
- Small wins keep you motivated.
- If you feel like procrastinating, **tell yourself to just start for 5 minutes.**
- Once you start, you'll likely continue.
- Put your **phone on silent** or in another room.
- Use apps that **block social media** while studying.
- Keep a note in front of you:
  "I am studying because I want to clear UPSC and build my future."
- When you feel like quitting, **read it and refocus.**
- I start even when I don't feel like it.
- I focus on **progress, not perfection.**
- I focus on **progress, not perfection.**
  I choose **discipline over temporary comfort.**

And that's how I am turning my dream into reality.

CHAPTER X

Finding True Happiness and Peace Within Yourself

"Happiness is not something you find outside. It is something you create within."

Why We Keep Searching for Happiness

For a long time, I believed happiness came from **external things**:

- Achieving success
- Receiving love and attention
- Having a perfect life without struggles

But even when I got what I wanted, the happiness was **temporary**. Soon, new desires, worries, and insecurities took over.

- I kept asking myself:
  "Why do I still feel incomplete? What am I missing?"

That's when I realized:
True happiness is not about what you have, but how you feel inside.

My Struggle: Depending on Others for Happiness

I used to feel happy only when:

- People appreciated me.
- I was surrounded by loved ones.
- Things in life were going perfectly.

But when things didn't go my way, I felt:

- Lonely and empty.
- Unhappy and restless.
- Like something was always missing.

This cycle continued until I understood that **happiness is an inside job.**

Story: The Man Who Searched for Happiness Everywhere

There was a man who spent years traveling the world, searching for happiness.

He visited beautiful places, met amazing people, and achieved great success. But still, he felt something was missing.

One day, an old monk told him:

"You are searching for happiness outside, but it has always been inside you."

That's when he realized that **peace and happiness come from within, not from the world outside.**

a. **Lesson:If you depend on external things for happiness, you will always feel incomplete. Learn to create peace within yourself.**

How to Find Happiness and Peace Within Yourself

1. Stop Seeking Validation from Others

- Your worth is **not defined by what others think of you.**
- Focus on self-growth, not external approval.

2. Be Present in the Moment

- Overthinking the past or future steals your peace.
- Learn to enjoy **what is happening right now.**

3. Accept Imperfections and Let Go of Control

- Life won't always go as planned, and that's okay.
- Instead of resisting, **accept, adapt, and move forward.**

4. Practice Gratitude Every Day

- Instead of focusing on what's missing, be grateful for what you have.
- Gratitude brings **instant peace and joy.**

Key Takeaways : Becoming Emotionally Independent

Now, I don't depend on people, situations, or achievements for happiness.

- I find joy in simple moments.
- I focus on **inner peace instead of external success.**
- I am happy, stable, and fulfilled—just by being myself.

And that is the true **art of peaceful success.**

Note Of Gratitude

This book is not just a collection of words—it is a reflection of my **journey, struggles, and lessons learned** while preparing for UPSC and navigating life's challenges.

I want to express my deep gratitude to:

- My **mentors and teachers** who guided me with knowledge and wisdom.
- My **family and friends** who supported me through thick and thin.
- The **difficult times** that taught me resilience, patience, and emotional strength.
- Every **mistake and failure** that shaped me into a wiser and more self-aware person.

Most importantly, I want to thank **myself**—for not giving up, for choosing growth over fear, and for striving to become a better version of who I was yesterday.

Final Words: A Note of Thanks

To every reader who picked up this book,
Thank you for allowing me to share my story with you.

I hope that my experiences, lessons, and real-life struggles help you:

- Stay strong in difficult times
- Build better relationships
- Overcome procrastination and self-doubt
- Find peace and happiness within yourself

Remember: **Your journey is unique, and every challenge is an opportunity to grow.**

No matter where you are in life, keep moving forward. Stay patient, stay positive, and trust yourself.

Success is not just about achieving goals—it's about becoming the best version of yourself while staying at peace.

With gratitude,

Vandana Singh